E
u

DATE DUE   2/08

MAR 1 7 2008			
NOV 1 5 2018			
MAY 0 9 2019			

DEMCO 38-296

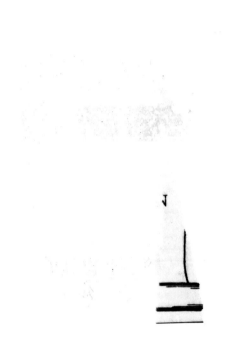

A Isn't for Fox

An Isn't Alphabet

Written by Wendy Ulmer and illustrated by Laura Knorr

A a

A isn't for box; it *isn't* for fox.

A is for ants that crawl over your socks.

B b

B isn't for kite; it isn't for light.
B is for bats that fly by in the night.

C c

C isn't for nap; it isn't for map.

C is for the cat curled up on your lap.

D d

D isn't for crow; it isn't for snow.
D is for dragons from times long ago.

G isn't for mugs; it isn't for bugs.
G is for geckos that hide on the rug.

Gg

H h

H isn't for rings; it isn't for strings.
H is for hummingbirds with whirring wings.

L isn't for dramas; it isn't for mamas.
L is for llamas in fuzzy pajamas.

L l

M isn't for rat; it isn't for bat.
M is for moose in a red-checkered hat.

M m

N n

N isn't for clown; it isn't for brown.

N is for nuthatch who walks upside down!

O isn't for docks; it isn't for rocks.
O is for octopus knitting four pairs of socks.

P isn't for goats; it isn't for boats.

P is for 'possums in warm, furry coats.

P p

Q isn't for towns; it isn't for frowns.
Q is for queen bees with lopsided crowns.

Qq

R r

R isn't for ear; it isn't for year.
R is for reindeer in backpacking gear.

S *isn't* for chair; it *isn't* for bear.
S is for salmon that leap through the air.

S s

T isn't for pies; it isn't for flies.
T is for turtles with purple bow ties.

T t

Uu

U isn't for teams; it isn't for streams.

U is for unicorn that visits in dreams.

V isn't for dove; it isn't for glove.
V is for vultures that watch from above.

W
W

W isn't for door; it isn't for snore.
W is for woodpecker whose bill is quite sore.

X isn't for seas; it isn't for peas.
X is for Xenops in rain forest trees.

Y y

Y isn't for fairy; it isn't for dairy.

Y is for yaks, chocolate brown and so hairy.

Z isn't for pipes; it isn't for wipes.
Z is for zebras with zig-zaggy stripes.

To my daughters, Amanda and Molly, with heartfelt thanks.

Wendy

☉

For Dad, with love.

Laura

Sleeping Bear Press™
310 North Main Street, Suite 300
Chelsea, MI 48118
www.sleepingbearpress.com

© 2008 Sleeping Bear Press is an imprint of Gale, a part of Cengage Learning.

Printed and bound in China.

First Edition

10 9 8 7 6 5 4 3 2 1

Library of Congress Cataloging-in-Publication Data

Ulmer, Wendy K., 1950-
A isn't for fox : an isn't alphabet / written by Wendy K. Ulmer ;
illustrated by Laura Knorr.
p. cm.
Summary: "Using humor and the alphabet this book points out first
what each letter of the alphabet is not for and then gives an example
of a word that does begin with the letter"—Provided by publisher.
ISBN 978-1-58536-319-3
1. Alphabet—Juvenile literature. I. Knorr, Laura, 1971- II. Title.
P211.U46 2007
[E]—dc22   2007006436